# I Can B

Written by Heather Drockelman, Ed.D.
Designed by Courtney Brown

There is a new area in my classroom with a real workbench.
There are tools, scraps of wood, a real hammer and wrench!

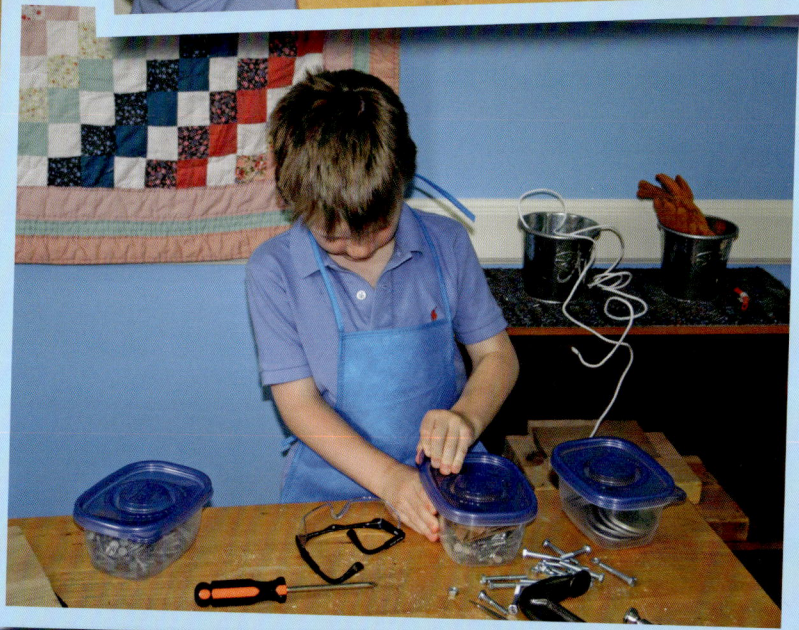

I want to get into those boxes to look and to find shapes of all different sizes, colors, and kinds.

There are gadgets and gizmos and stuff that is fitting,
some of this and some of that and even stuff that was missing.

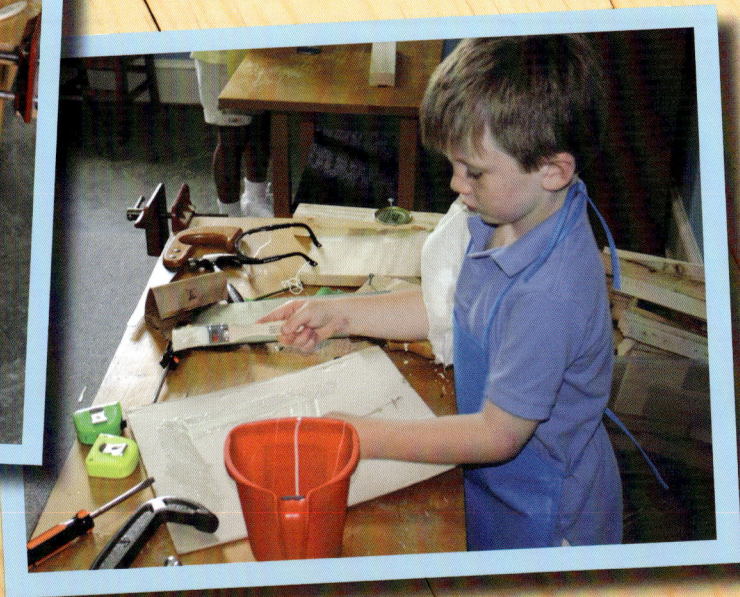

There is so much to make and so much to do.
I have plans! I have ideas! I'll use this stuff and some glue.

I choose the biggest pieces of wood and lay them on the table. If I put down the heaviest ones first, my building will be more stable.

The glue is a little drippy, but I finally get it to stick.
Holding it and counting to ten does the trick.

If I put this piece of wood on top, it looks like a bridge or second floor. I can glue this smaller piece here, like that, to make it look like a door.

My ideas are changing; I sure have a lot.
I can build a house or a boat or a castle. Why not?

But then I hear it, plain as day.
"Time to clean up," I hear my teacher say.

I was just getting started. I'm not ready to go.
I want to build and finish my creation, you know.

But then she kindly says, "You're really making progress.
You can have time to work on it later. Let's just clean up this mess."